Where Are You?

bedroom

bathroom

living room

dining room

laundry room

kitchen

basement

garage

Where are you?

I'm in the bathroom.

Where are you?

I'm in the
bedroom.

Where are you?

I'm in the kitchen.

Where are you?

I'm in the dining room.

Where are you?

I'm in the living room.

Where are you?

I'm in the laundry room.

Let's learn more about Brazil.

Feijoada